Colorful Batik

PANEL QUILTS

28 Quilting & Embellishing Inspirations from Around the World

by Judith Vincentz Gula

Colorful Batik Panel Quilts
by Judith Vincentz Gula

Landauer Publishing (www.landauerpub.com) is an imprint of Fox Chapel Publishing Company, Inc.

Copyright © 2019 by Judith Vincentz Gula and Fox Chapel Publishing Company, Inc.
903 Square Street, Mount Joy, PA 17552.

Project Team:
Vice President-Content: Christopher Reggio
Editors: Laurel Albright/Sue Voegtlin
Copy Editor: Katie Ocasio
Designer: Laurel Albright
Photographer: Sue Voegtlin

ISBN: 978-1-947163-05-8

Library of Congress Control Number: 2018959790

We are always looking for talented authors.
To submit an idea, please send a brief inquiry to acquisitions@foxchapelpublishing.com.

Printed in Singapore

21 20 19 18   2 4 6 8 10 9 7 5 3 1

This book has been published with the intent to provide accurate and authoritative information in regard to the subject matter within. While every precaution has been taken in the preparation of this book, the author and publisher expressly disclaim any responsibility for any errors, omissions, or adverse effects arising from the use or application of the information contained herein.

Table of Contents

Introduction

The Indonesian batik art panels in this book are wonderfully beautiful and executed by experienced men and women artists in Java and other parts of Indonesia. I have come to love the art created by these incredibly talented artists, becoming quite passionate about the creation of batik art panels. We hope that you will join us in this journey to Indonesia.

The Fair Trade Movement

Seven years ago, my husband, Dave, and I merged our business, Artistic Artifacts, with Batik Tambal. This allowed us to expand our product offerings to include Indonesian Batik Panels. Owners of Batik Tambal, Trish & Owen Hodge brought this wonderful textile art with them to the US from Indonesia over 20 years ago.

We are a part of the "Fair Trade" movement, and we pay the asking price for the panels. In doing so, we have created long-term relationships with these talented artists. By purchasing these panels, we are helping provide a living wage to them, their families, and in turn, their communities.

Batik Artists

Batik is an art form of intricate design and brilliant colors, and the fabrics depict the culture and environment of the island.

Indonesia has a heritage of rich textiles and on the island of Java, batiks, a dye and wax resist process, has risen to a standard of the highest quality. Our batik artists are men who continue to work with fine art mediums, including life size acrylic paintings and panel designs. Some teach in universities and are a part of the launching of this "new" art form.

The panels are completed in a cooperative environment of workshops in their homes. Women create the panel details, following decades of old tradition. This practice was regarded as an important part of a young woman's accomplishment to be capable of applying the fine detail often seen in Batik cloth.

Batik Panels

Batik is a technique of wax-resist and dyeing. Starting with a freehand sketch or an illustration traced onto white, tightly woven cotton fabric, a canting tool, shown here, is used to apply wax in lines and dots. The wax resists the dye as color is applied to the fabric. The wax is removed with boiling water, and the process can be repeated to add additional colors.

The finished panels come to us pressed and ready to incorporate into our artwork. We think of it as a long distance partnership between the Indonesian artist and the artist who incorporates it into their artwork, quilts, or clothing.

A panel can be any piece of fabric that you especially love. Fabric companies sometimes create panels along with their collections. This may be seasonal, specific to a theme, or a creation of the designer's inspiration.

The panels in this book focus on those created by the artists of Indonesia. I love the artistry and detail in them. Using these panels in my creations has become a passion of mine.

Whatever you choose, any of the following techniques can be applied to your panel choice.

Border Inspirations

SQUARING UP THE PANEL

Batik panels are manipulated and washed many times before being used in a project. Squaring up the panel is important, especially if you plan on adding borders to it.

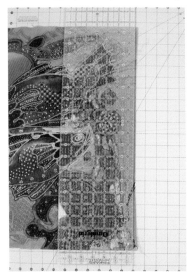 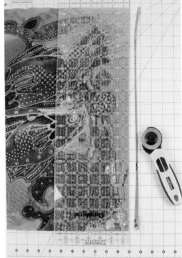 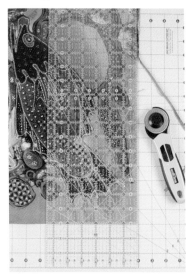

1 Press the panel and lay flat on a cutting mat. Lay a ruler along one edge of the panel. Square up the edge of the ruler along a vertical and horizontal line of the mat.

2 Determine how much of the panel you want to trim. Pull the panel fabric beyond the edge of the squared-up ruler and trim.

3 Rotate the panel and realign the ruler on a vertical and horizontal line of the mat as shown. Repeat step 2 to trim a second side of the panel.

4 Continue rotating and realigning the ruler to square up all sides of the panel.

WONKY PANELS

Rather than trimming the sides of the panel straight, you can trim the sides at a bit of an angle to create a wonky panel. I like to start by laying my ruler even with one corner of the panel and adjust the opposite edge 1/4" (0.64cm) to 3/4" (1.91cm) off to "unsquare" my panel.

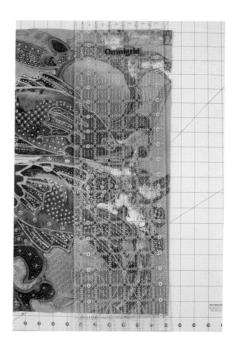

CHOOSING BORDER COLORS

To complement a Batik panel, you can choose border colors from within the panel, using either solids or prints. You can preview your fabric choices by folding the fabric and laying it against the panel. Try folding different widths, too. There is no right or wrong color or width to a border.

Adding Borders

Borders can be added to a panel in any number and in any width you choose. Because panels vary in size, you can use the following instructions to cut borders with confidence.

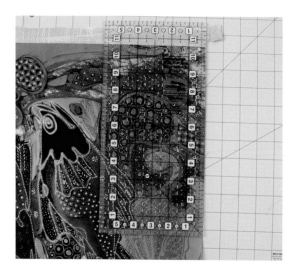

1 Choose which sides of the panel you want to add borders to first. Measure and cut 2 strips, adding a little extra fabric.

2 Center a strip along each side and sew using a 1/4" (0.64cm) seam. Trim the strips even with panel. Measure the remaining 2 sides of panel, including borders, adding a little extra fabric. Cut the strips and center each to a remaining side. Sew and trim even to square the up panel.

As you add borders, alternate the addition of strips to make stepped corners.

Your borders don't have to be the same width. In this project the bottom is 2" to 3" (5 to 7.62cm) wider. It shows an entire leaf-like batik design, which is why I chose to make the bottom border a bit bigger.

FLANGED BORDERS

To add some dimension, try making a flange to border the panel.

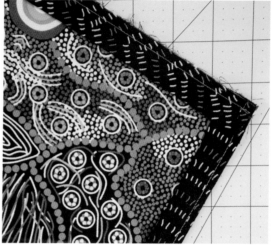

1 Determine the finished width of the flange. Double the size and add 1/2" (1.27cm) to this measurement. For instance, if the finished size is 1/2" (1.27cm), double it to 1" (2.54cm) and add and extra 1/2" (1.27cm) for the seam allowance. Press the strip wrong sides together.

2 Measure a side of the panel and cut a flange strip to length plus a little extra. Align and center the raw edge of the flange to edge of panel and sew using a 1/4" (0.64cm) seam. Repeat for additional sides.

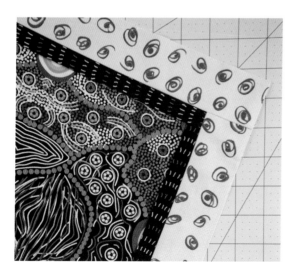

3 You can add additional borders to flange, and a flange can be sewn anywhere within any border.

MAKING A PIANO KEYS BORDER

I love using this technique to border a panel. I like to mix lights and darks, patterned strips and solids and it's a great way to use up scraps. Jelly roll strips are easy to use but your border strips will be all the same width. And that's okay! This is your project and there's plenty of opportunity to make it your own.

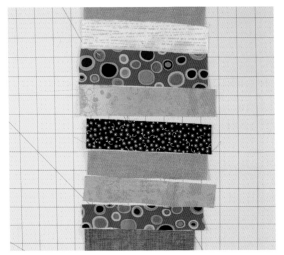

1 This border idea can be used with any size panel. The width of the border strip sets will change with the size of the panel. Experiment with strip set widths before attaching it to your panel.

2 The scrappy keys for this border are made from a variety of pieced cotton strips. Use a combination of lights and darks from batiks, prints, and solids. Strips can vary from 1" (2.54cm) to 2" (5.08cm) wide. Don't worry if the strips aren't even; the randomness adds interest to the border.

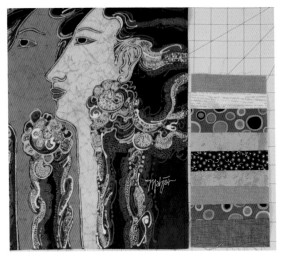

3 Before I sew strip sets together, I like to lay them out and get an idea of color placement. It makes sewing them together much faster since I've already created a color order.

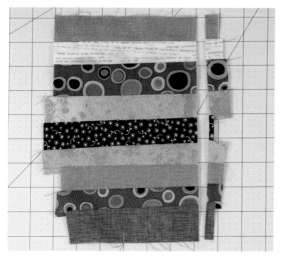

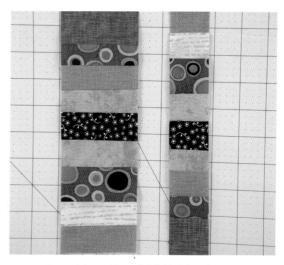

 Before attaching to the panel, press the seams in one direction. Square up one side of the strip set to align with the panel.

5 Sew strips with a 1/4" (0.64cm) seam allowance to make a long strip set. Cut the strip sets to the desired width.

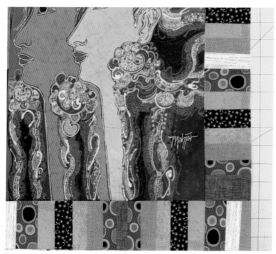

 Measure two sides of your panel. Sew strip sets together to equal this number. (It's okay to trim to size if necessary). Sew with 1/4" (0.64cm) seam allowance. Repeat for all the sides of the panel.

If you want to add cornerstones, measure the top/bottom and sides of panel from corner to corner. Attach generous squares to two ends of two strips. Sew these strips on last and trim to square up the panel.

Silk Keys

I received a small package of Indian silk sari fabrics and used them to border this panel for an elegant addition to these Indonesian ladies. I wasn't sure how to sew the silk to the cotton, so my solution was to back the silk with a single-sided, knit, fusible interfacing. My favorite is Mistyfuse®. It gives the silk or any fine or loose weave fabric a bit of stability when you sew strips together.

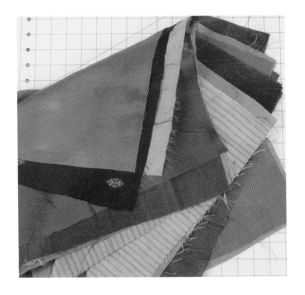

1 I use the same process to make a silk border as a cotton border. Follow the manufacturer's instructions to apply interfacing to silk fabric pieces or strips before you sew. Lay out your strips before you start to sew to relieve the stress of fretting over which color to sew next!

2 I like to chain piece sets of 4 to 6 strips at one time. I press the seams in one direction and then sew the sets together to add to my panel.

"Sisters" by batik artist Bambang Dharmo

CORNERSTONES

If you want to add cornerstones, measure the top, bottom and sides of the panel from corner to corner. Attach generous squares to two ends of two strips. Sew these strips on last and trim to square up the panel.

EASY PIANO KEYS

If you like the look of a pieced border but don't want to spend the time piecing multiple strips, try making a border from striped fabric. In this panel, the border fabric created a nice finish very similar to a pieced border.

FINISHING YOUR PANEL

Finishing a panel is really no different than finishing a quilt. The top, batting, and backing are layered and pin-basted. The binding is sewn to the front and turned to the back to be stitched down by hand.

A Traditional Finish

An easy way to finish the project is to simply quilt your panel in the traditional way. The process is simple. Layer the backing, batting and panel top. Secure with pins and quilt by hand or machine.

1 Press your panel and measure the width and length.

2 Cut a piece of batting and backing, adding 2" (5.08cm) to 4" (10.16cm) to measurements.

3 Layer backing, wrong side up, then batting. Gently smooth out the pieces. If the batting is wrinkled, toss it in the dryer for a few minutes.

4 Layer the panel on top of the batting, making sure there is backing and batting showing on all sides of the panel. Pin-baste or use basting stitches through all layers. Quilt as desired.

Embellished Finish

To add embellishments like beads, charms, buttons or hand stitching, it's important to stabilize your panel before you start. I use a w piece of flannel and Mistyfuse® interfacing to adhere to my panel. It keeps the stitches and beading secure on the panel front. Whatever you use, follow the manufacturer's instructions when you're ready to layer the panel and flannel. After embellishing, following the steps for a traditional finish.

Log Cabin Blocks ⬥ · · · · · · · · · · · · · · · · · ·

It's easy to apply this step-by-step to any size panel you use and the panel can be square or rectangular in shape. If you're making a quilt using log cabin blocks, you may need to construct the blocks first and then work their unfinished size into your quilt pattern.

LOG CABIN BLOCKS

For a structured log cabin block, start with a center square then add logs in a clockwise rotation. Before you start, determine the width of your strips. You can cut width-of-fabric strips, use Jelly Roll strips, or use up scraps. Logs don't have to match. They can be pieced or you can alternate light and dark logs for contrast. Follow the illustration to add logs around your center square.

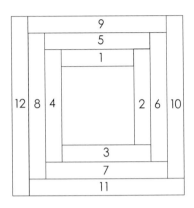

1 Measure the side of your panel in the #1 position. Cut a strip to this size plus a little extra. Sew the strip to the square using a 1/4" (0.64cm) seam and trim any extra. Press the seam away from square.

2 Measure the side of your panel in the #2 position, including the first log. Add a little extra and cut and sew the strip to this side. Trim any extra.

3 Measure the side, including the width of the #2 strip and repeat steps 1 to 2. Measure the side, including the width of the #3 strip and repeat steps 1 to 2 to complete the first round of logs.

4 Continue adding logs in this manner. Square up the block if necessary.

WONKY LOG CABIN BLOCKS

Strips for a wonky Log Cabin block can be 1 1/2" to 2" (3.81 to 5.08cm) wide by the generous length of a side of your squared block. When trimming, angle the ruler to cut an uneven log, making sure to trim no less than 1/2" to 3/4" (1.27 to 2cm) from a seam. Not sticking to any one measurement or angle as you trim will give your finished block more visual variety.

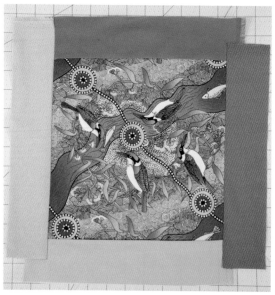

1 Using four identical-width strips, sew a log to each side of your panel.

2 Angle a ruler and trim each log within 1/2" to 3/4" (1.27 to 2cm) from any edge.

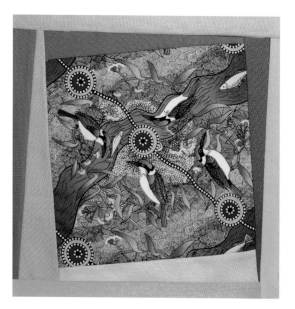

3 Continue sewing and trimming rounds, referring to step 1. You can add as many rounds as you like. When you are finished adding logs, square up the block making sure to leave 1/4" (0.64cm) seam allowance.

"School of Fish" by batik artist Jaka

Embellishing Inspirations

WITH HAND STITCHES, BEADS, BUTTONS, CHARMS

One of the most basic ways to embellish is with hand stitches but embellishing doesn't stop there! You can add beads, buttons, charms, ribbons, delicate skeleton leaves, dyed doilies, or anything you can imagine.

Things You'll Need

- Sewing Machine
- Scissors
- Sewing Needles
- Threads
- Yarns
- Beads
- Glue
- Metal Stampings and Findings
- Doilies
- Skeleton Leaves
- Collected Bits & Pieces

TIP

Always begin by threading the needle and knotting the thread. Bring the needle and thread up from the back to the front of the fabric.

STRAIGHT STITCH

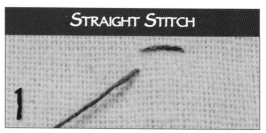

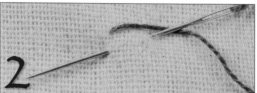

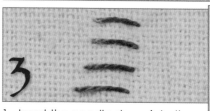

back of fabric

1. Insert the needle down into the fabric where you want your first stitch to end. Bring the needle back up to the top of the fabric at the beginning of the second stitch.

2. Pull the thread through in one motion. Don't pull the stitch too tight or it will cause the fabric to bunch.

3. Continue stitching in the same manner. When you are finished stitching, take the needle and thread to the back of the fabric and knot. Stitches on the back and front of the fabric will be similar.

RUNNING STITCH

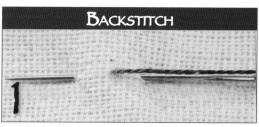

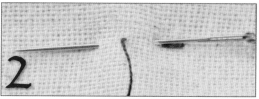

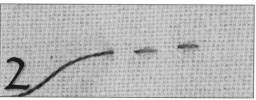

BACKSTITCH

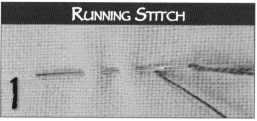

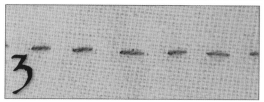

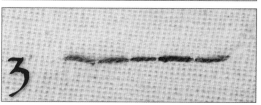

1. Bring the needle in and out of the fabric, loading three to four stitches on it. Stitches and spaces between stitches should be equal in length.

2. Pull the needle and thread through the fabric, taking care not to pull the thread too tight.

3. Continue stitching in the same manner. When you are finished stitching, take the needle and thread to the back of the fabric and knot.

1. Insert the needle one stitch length behind, or to the right of where the thread exited the fabric. Bring the needle up one stitch length, or to the left, of where the thread exited the fabric.

2. Pull the thread through the fabric for the first stitch. Insert the needle in the end of the stitch length to the left, or in front, of the thread. This is a "two steps forward and one step back" motion.

3. Continue stitching in the same manner until the line of stitches is your desired length. To finish, take the needle and thread to the back of the fabric and knot.

STEM STITCH

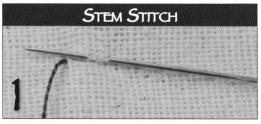

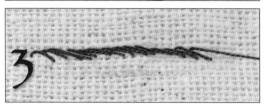

BLANKET STITCH

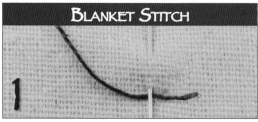

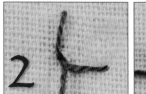 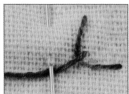

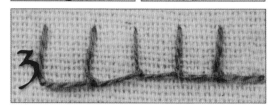

1. Take the needle tip down into the fabric and come up just above and to the right of the thread exit. Pull the thread through the fabric to create the first stitch.

2. For the second stitch, insert the needle one stitch length to the right of the first stitch. Keep the tip of needle in line with the end of the last stitch, bringing the needle halfway up and beside the first stitch.

3. Continue stitching in the same manner until your line of stitches is the desired length.

1. Insert the needle where you want the first stitch to end, approximately 1/4" (0.64cm) in front of the beginning of the first stitch at a right angle. Keep the thread under the needle.

2. Pull through to make and "L." Continue stitching in the same manner.

3. When you are finished with the blanket stitch, take the thread to the back and knot.

DETACHED CROSS STITCH

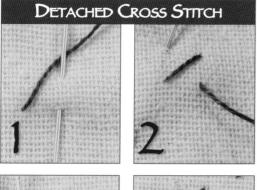

Use this stitch to make random crosses.

1. Knot the thread and bring the needle up from the wrong side the of fabric where you want the first stitch to start. Insert the needle into the fabric to the right of the thread exit to create a diagonal stitch.

2. Cross back over the first stitch and insert the needle into the fabric to create an "X," while bringing the needle back where the next stitch is to be placed.

3. Continue making detached cross stitches.

4. When you are finished stitching, take the thread to the back and knot.

DETACHED FEATHER STITCH

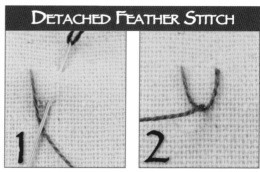
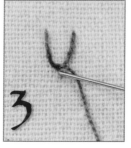
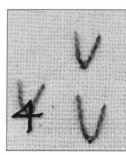

1. Knot the thread and bring the needle up from the wrong side of the fabric where you want the first stitch to start. Insert the needle approximately 1/4" (0.64cm) to the right of the thread exit, bringing the needle back up in the center and below the stitch to form a "V."

2. Loop the thread under the needle and pull through.

3. Insert the needle right below the bottom of the "V" as close as you can to complete the stitch. In one motion, you can insert the needle and bring it back up to where you want the second stitch to start.

4. Continue making random feather stitches. If the stitches are too far apart, you may want to knot each one separately.

SEED STITCH

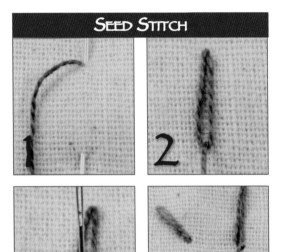

FLY STITCH

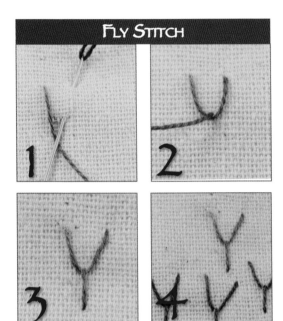

1. Knot the thread and bring the needle up from the wrong side of the fabric where you want the first stitch to start. Insert the needle back down into the fabric close to the thread exit. Bring the needle back up to the top of fabric below the first stitch and loop the thread under the needle. The seed length can be any length you choose.

2. Pull the needle through to the front.

3. Secure the stitch by inserting the needle down into the fabric just outside the loop.

4. Continue making a series of seed stitches. When you are finished, take the thread to the back and knot.

1. Knot the thread and bring the needle up from the wrong side of fabric where you want the first stitch to start. Insert the needle approximately 1/4" (0.64cm) to the right or left of the thread exit, bringing the needle back up in the center to form a "V."

2. Loop the thread under the needle and pull through.

3. Insert the needle 1/4" (0.64cm) below the "V" to form a "Y." In one motion, you can insert the needle to where you want the second stitch to start.

4. Continue making random fly stitches. If the stitches are too far apart, you may want to knot each one separately.

FRENCH KNOT

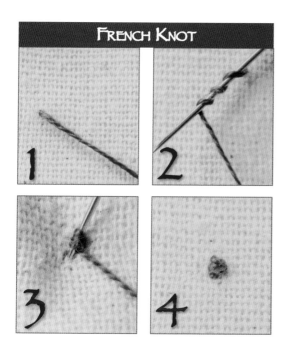

RICE STITCH

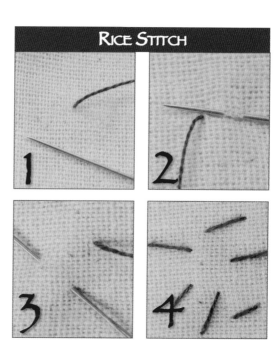

1. Knot the thread and bring the needle up from the wrong side of the fabric where you want the first stitch to start.

2. Wrap the thread around the needle one to three times.

3. Insert the needle into the fabric as close as possible to where the thread exits. Slide the wrapped thread down to the fabric with your thumb.

4. Pull the thread straight through to the back of the fabric. Do not let go of the wrapped thread until it is snugged up to the fabric, creating the knot.

1. Knot the thread and bring the needle up from the wrong side of the fabric where you want the first stitch to start.

2. Take a 1/4" (0.635cm) to 1/3" (0.85cm) stitch in any direction. Bring the needle up where you want the next stitch to begin.

3. Pull the needle through and take another stitch in another direction, keeping the stitch length fairly consistent.

4. Continue stitching in the same manner until the area is covered. When you are finished, take the thread to the back and knot.

Beading on panels is one of my favorite embellishing techniques. Beads and crystals can add sparkle and texture to enhance the design of the panel and make it your own piece of art. Single stitch and backstitch are the two techniques I use the most.

SINGLE STITCH

This stitch makes a highlight dot or it can be used as a textural element.

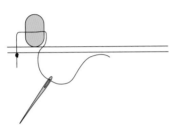

Knot the thread and bring up the needle at the starting point. String a single bead. Reinsert the needle next to the bead and come back up through the fabric at the point of the next stitch; repeat as desired.

NOTE: If the stitches are fairly far apart knot off the thread between each stitch.

BACKSTITCH

This is used to make a long line of beads and is great for outlining shapes or objects.

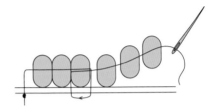

1 Knot the thread and bring the needle up at the starting point. Tug on the thread to pop the knot into the batting. String three (size 8 or larger) or five (size 11) beads onto the thread. Holding the thread taut, gently push the beads back with the needle so they press against the fabric at the starting point. Reinsert the needle into the quilt right behind the last bead so the beads do not gap (too long of a distance) or pucker (too short of a distance).

2 Take a small backstitch, backing up one bead if you strung three, or two beads if you strung five, taking care not to pierce the thread. Go through the last previously laid bead(s), then add three to five more beads to the thread and repeat from the beginning of this step until the line is completed; knot off.

Add novelty to your panel with unique items that take your panel into a decorative work of art. Use embellishments that have special meaning to you such as old buttons, metal stampings, charms, found objects, and doilies.

METAL STAMPINGS, CHARMS

I like to embellish my projects with metal stamps and charms. It can add a message and movement to create beautiful art quilts.

DOILIES

Vintage doilies are one of my favorite embellishments. They can easily transform an art panel into a three-dimensional wonder without overwhelming the focus on the panel!

I hand dye vintage dollies in an array of colors and keep a stash in my studio.

SKELETON LEAVES AND SEQUINS

Add a skeleton leaf or sequins to your batik art quilt to add texture and dimension that reaches out beyond the fabric surface.

Using a sewing machine to add beautiful detail to your panel with free-motion quilting designs will enhance the design of the artwork.

OUTLINE & ECHO QUILTING

A beautiful panel with simple shapes lends itself to outline quilting (see left image).

Echo quilting is done easily within the abstract design of a border (see right image).

Intuitive Quilting

Panels with hidden designs can be brought to life with outline quilting. Imagine a bird fluttering around the flowers. If you look closely you'll see it in the quilting.

FILL SHAPES

I love the leaves in the plants Mahyar draws! I filled the leaves and trees with stitching to add detail to them.

MEANDERING

Many of these panels have open spaces that are perfect for meander quilting. The soft "S" curves give the space dimension and movement.

SWIRLS

Swirls are a great overall design. The fluidity of the swirls help draw attention to the artwork in Rusli's panels without overwhelming them.

PEBBLING

Pebbling is a wonderful way to add texture to solid color areas of the panels.

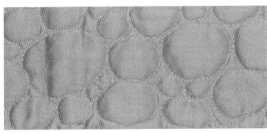

MACHINE QUILTING

I like to add my own touch to the panels with detail machine quilting. Stitching flowers or filling the heart shape adds another dimension to the artwork.

Projects & Gallery Tour

No two finished panels will ever be the same because the goal is to make your project reflect your choices in color and embellishment. We stitch differently, quilt differently, and apply our personal vision and creativity to everything we make. Be fearless and create as you go. No right or wrong, no rules, and no inhibitions to stop you.

The instructions for the quilts are a basic guide to follow but don't be alarmed if your blocks aren't exactly the measurements given. As long as they are all the same size, adjustments can be made to sashing and borders.

Your panel may vary in size but step-by-step instructions for construction, stitches, and other embellishments can be applied with small changes on your part to accommodate measurements.

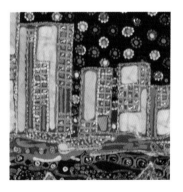

Project created by Judith Vincentz Gula
Longarm quilting by Judy Hendrickson

Woman with Crown

Approximately 67" x 72" (1.70 x 1.83m)

Jaka is one of our most prolific and respected batik designers. The bright and bold colors inspire a wonderful log cabin block quilt. The center panel should measure 36-1/2" x 41-1/2" (0.93 x 1.05m) and I have left it up to you to create it. Blocks and border measurements are based on this panel size. Refer to quilt photo for color inspiration

Materials

3/4 yard (0.70m) fabric for borders.
Cut 4" (10.16cm) x WOF strips.
Sew strips end to end and cut:

(2) 4" x 72-1/5" (10.16 x 185.42cm)
side border strips

(2) 4" x 66" (10.16 x 154.94cm)
top and bottom strips

4 yards (8.87m) backing and batting

1/2 yard (0.46m) binding fabric (0.46m)

General Instructions

- Width of fabric is 42" (1.06m).
- Seams are sewn using 1/4" (0.64cm).

Making the Quilt

Center Panel
Refer to Squaring Up The Panel, page 10, and Adding Borders, page 12. Sew borders to panel to make a center panel, 36-1/2" x 41-1/2" (0.93 x 1.05m). Press seams away from the center.

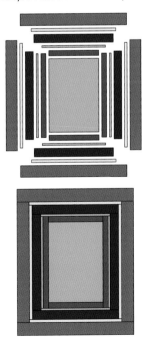

Log Cabin Blocks

Refer to Squaring Up the Panel, page 10, and Making Log Cabin blocks, page 20. Your log cabin center can be any size you want as long as the block measures 12-1/2" (31.75cm) square. Make (12) 12-1/2" (31.75cm) blocks.

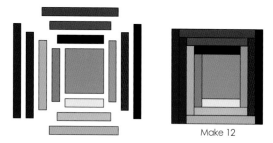

Make 12

Additional Blocks

Referring to the quilt photo on page 38, assemble (4) 15" x 12-1/2" (38.1 x 31.75cm) blocks. These blocks can be any combination of a center square and any number of borders as long as they meet the required measurement.

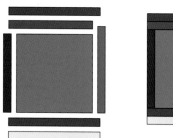 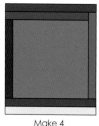

Make 4

Quilt Assembly

1. Lay out quilt blocks as shown in Quilt Assembly Diagram. Sew blocks together in vertical and horizontal rows. Press seams.

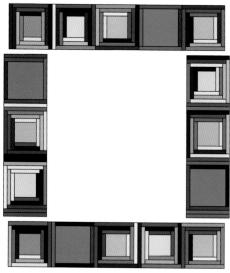

Quilt Assembly Diagram

2. Sew vertical rows to either side of the center panel. Press seams away from the center.

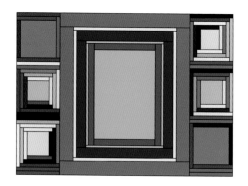

3. Sew horizontal rows to top and bottom of the quilt center and press the seams away from the center.

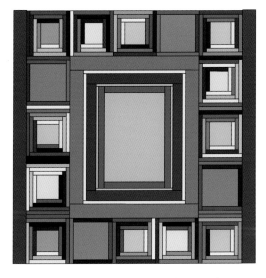

4. Sew borders to either side of the quilt center. Sew the top and bottom borders to the quilt and press seams away from the center.

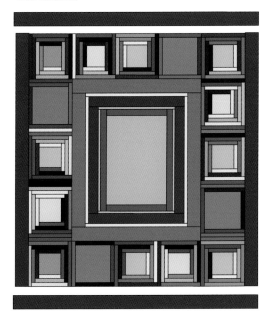

Finishing the Quilt

1. Layer backing, batting, and quilt top. Quilt as desired.

2. Cut 2-1/2" (6.35cm) strips from binding fabric and sew together end to end, to make one long binding strip. Press seams open.

3. Press strips with wrong sides together. Sew to front of the quilt along raw edges. Fold binding the back, covering raw edges, and hand stitch in place.

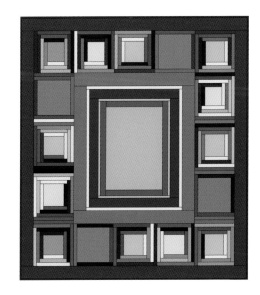

Project created by Judith Vincentz Gula
Longarm quilting by Judy Hendrickson

⊹ Rusli Meets Milo ⊹

Approximately 68" x 84" (1.73 x 2.13m)

This quilt is named after the artist, Rusli, who created the center panels. They arrived at the shop approximately 12" (30.48cm) square with a 1-1/2" (3.81cm) white border surrounding the batik design. The panels were squared to 9-1/2" (24.13cm). Because of the irregularity of the panels, some of the white border is visible. This doesn't bother me but you can make your panels a bit smaller if you'd like. Sashing was added to make 15-1/2" (39.37cm)blocks. This is a very scrappy quilt with block sashing sometimes pieced to accommodate a side of the panel.

Materials

(12) 9-1/2" (24.13cm) square panels
   for block centers

1-5/8 yard (1.48m) for panel frames

1/2 yard (45.72cm) black print fabric
   for quilt center sashing

5/8 yard (57.15cm) print
   for outer sashing

1-1/2 yard (1.37m) print fabric
   for borders

5 yards (4.57m)
   for backing and batting

3/4 yards (0.70m) for binding

Cutting Instructions

From 1-5/8 yard (1.48m) assorted print strip fabric, cut:

(12) 3-1/2" x 9-1/2" (8.89 x 24.13cm)
strips or assorted pieces to equal strip size

(24) 3-1/2" x 12-1/2" (8.89 x 31.75cm)
strips or assorted pieces to equal strip size

(12) 3-1/2" x 15-1/2" (8.89 x 39.37cm)
strips or assorted pieces to equal strip size

From 1/2 yard (45.72cm) black print fabric, cut:

(6) 1-1/2" x WOF strips. Sew strips end to end and cut:
   (4) 1-1/2" x 64" (3.81cm x 1.62m) strips
   (2) 1-1/2" x 51" (3.81cm x 1.29m)
   (9) 1-1/2" x 16" (3.81 x 40.64cm)

From 5/8 yard (.58m) print fabric, cut:

(6) 3-1/2" (8.89cm) x WOF strips.
   Sew strips end to end and cut:
   (2) 3-1/2" x 67" (8.89cm x 1.70m) strips
   for side sashing
   (2) 3-1/2" x 57" (8.89cm x 1.44m) for top and
   bottom sashing

From 1-1/2 yards (1.83m) print fabric, cut:

(7) 7" (17.78cm) x WOF strips. Sew strips end to
   end and cut:
   (2) 7" x 69" (17.78cm x 1.75m) print strips for
   top and bottom border
   (2) 7" x 72" (17.78cm x 1.83m) print strips
   for side borders

Making the Blocks

1. Following the instructions (page 10), square up panels to make (12) 9-1/2" (24.13cm) block centers.

2. For EACH block center, sew a 3-1/2" x 9-1/2" (8.89cm x 24.13cm) strip to the top side of the panel. Press seams away from center.

3. Working clockwise: Sew (1) 3-1/2" x 12-1/2" (8.89cm x 31.75cm) strip (this may be a pieced strip) to the right side, (1) 3-1/2" x 12-1/2" (8.89cm x 31.75cm) strip to the bottom side, and (1) 3-1/2" x 15-1/2" (8.89cm x 39.37cm) to the left side. Press seams away from the center. Make (12) blocks.

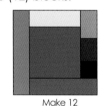

Make 12

Quilt Assembly

1. Lay out four rows of (3) blocks. Sew a 1-1/2" x 16" (3.81 x 40.64cm) strip to bottom of the first three blocks in each vertical row.

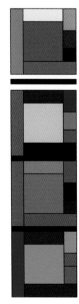

2. On the left side of the first vertical row, sew a 1-1/2" x 64" (3.81cm x 1.62m) strip. Sew the additional 1-1/2" x 64" (3.81cm x 1.62m) strips to join the vertical rows, ending with 1 strip on the right side of the third vertical row. Trim strips even with rows.

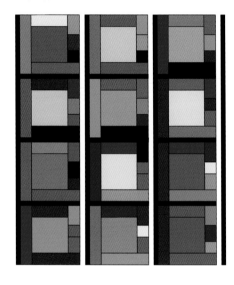

3. Sew a 1-1/2" x 51" (3.81 x 1.29m) strip to the top and bottom of the quilt center. Trim strips even.

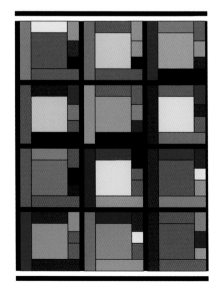

4. Sew a 3-1/2" x 67" (8.89 x 1.70m) pieced strip to each side of the assembled quilt center.

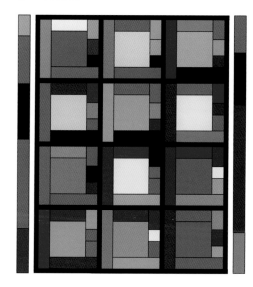

5. Sew a 3-1/2" x 57" (8.89cm x 1.44m) pieced strip to the top and bottom of the quilt center.

6. Sew a 7" x 72" (17.78cm x 1.83m) print border strip to each side of the quilt center.

7. Sew a 7" x 69" (17.78c x 1.75m) print border strip to top and bottom of the quilt center.

Finishing the Quilt

1. Layer backing, batting, and quilt top. Quilt as desired.

2. Cut 2-1/2" (6.35cm) strips from binding fabric and sew together end to end to make one long binding strip. Press seams open.

3. Press the strips wrong sides together. Sew to the front of quilt along raw edges. Fold the binding to the back of the quilt, covering raw the edges, and hand stitch in place.

Project created by Judith Vincentz Gula

·✦· School of Fish ·✦·

Approximately 42" x 63" (1.07 x 1.60m)

This panel by Jaka is inspired by the beautiful wildlife that inhabits Indonesia. The fun caricatures of the fish make it perfect for a wonky log cabin quilt. By trimming the fish panels unevenly, it enhanced the movement of the fish, especially when wonky strips were added around the panel. If you want, you can square up each panel and add wonky strips or log cabin logs. Just make sure your blocks finish 9-1/2" (24.13cm) square.

Materials

(20) 5-1/2" (13.97cm) various squares
    for center of block

5/8 yard (0.57m) black/white print
    for borders

1/2 yard (0.46m) blue batik for sashing

2-1/2 yards (2.30m)
    for backing and batting

1/2 yard (0.46m) for binding

General Instructions

Width of fabric is 42" (1.07m). Seams are sewn using a 1/4" (0.64cm).

Wonky logs: 3 to 5 strips were sewn around each square. You may use more or less strips, depending on how wide your strips are and how wonky you cut them.

Cutting Instructions

From panels or fussy cut fabric, cut:
(20) 5-1/2" (13.97cm) squares

From black and white print, cut:
(17) 1-1/4" (3.18cm) strips.
    Sew strips end to end to make:
    (2) 59" (1.50m) inner side sashing strips
    (10) 37" (0.94m) strips for row sashings

    (2) 64" (1.63m) side border strips
    (2) 43" (1.09m) top/bottom border strips

From the blue batik, cut:
(9) 2" (5.08cm) x WOF strips.
    Sew strips end to end to make:
    (2) 37" (0.94m) strips for row sashings
    (2) 42" (1.07m) top/bottom sashing strips
    (2) 59" (1.50cm) side sashing strips

Making the Blocks

Referring to instructions on page 22, add logs to the sides of (20) 5-1/2" (13.97cm). Logs can be 1-1/2" x 2" (3.81 x 5.08cm) in width. Cut the length with a little extra fabric. Depending on how you want your block to look, you can piece the logs, use scraps, or cut from selected yardage. Blocks should measure 9-1/2" (24.13cm) square.

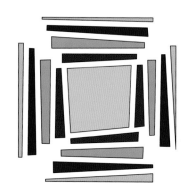

Putting the Quilt Together

Sashing and border strips are generous. Trim even as strips are attached.

1. Lay the blocks out in five rows of (4) blocks. Sew rows together using a 1/4" (0.64cm) seam. Press seams open or to one side.

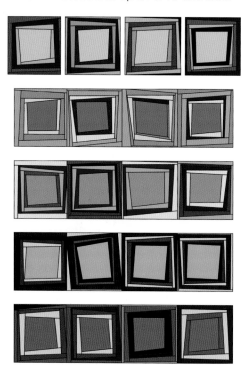

2. Sew the (10) black/white 37" (0.94m) strips to the top and bottom of block rows.

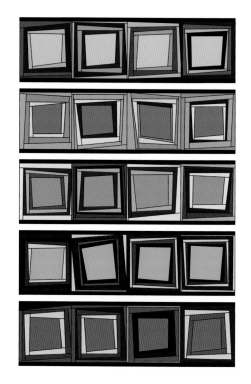

3. Sew the (4) 37" (0.94m) blue batik strips in between rows to make the quilt center.

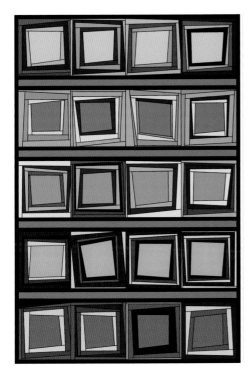

4. Sew the (2) 59" (1.50m) black/white inner side sashing strips to the sides of the quilt center.

5. Sew the (2) 59" (1.50m) blue batik side sashing strips to each side of the quilt center.

6. Sew the (2) 42" (1.07m) blue batik sashing strips to top/bottom of the quilt center.

7. Sew the (2) 43" (1.09m) black/white print strips to the top and bottom of the quilt center.

8. Sew the (2) 64" (1.63m) black/white print strips to the outer side borders.

Finishing the Quilt

1. Layer backing, batting, and quilt top. Quilt as desired.

2. Cut 2-1/2" (6.35cm) strips from the binding fabric and sew together end to end to make one long binding strip. Press seams open.

3. Press strips wrong sides together. Sew to front of quilt along raw edges. Fold the binding to the back of the quilt, covering the raw edges, and hand stitch in place.

Batik Flowers

Panel by Hari Agung
Project created by Judith Vincentz Gula

Judy's Way of Design

  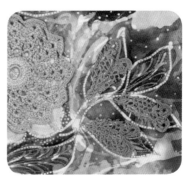

DOILIES

I pulled several doilies in different colors and laid them on the quilt. I wanted to keep the batik art quilt as the main focal point; dollies need to add some texture but not take over. Pinning my choices in place, careful not to sew over the pins, I used thread that matched the dollies and free motion stitched them in place. Sometimes whole dollies were used; other times, cut pieces.

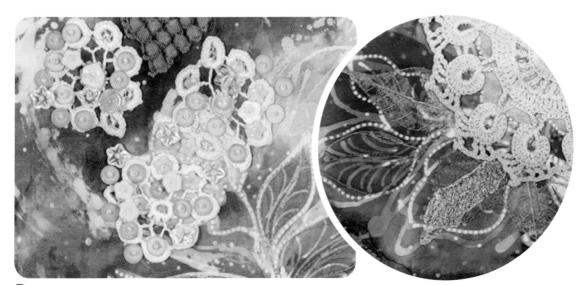

BEADING

My idea was to use a variety of beads and stitching to create a Hydrangea-type flower. I used the beading to extend beyond the doily and batik flower. And sometimes, all that is needed is to just keep it simple! In the top left doily, I added beads to the center of my vintage doily "flower."

SKELETON LEAVES

I like to use Skeleton Leaves to embellish the batik art quilts. It adds texture and dimension that reaches out beyond the fabric surface.

Artistic Artifacts Meets Batik Tambal

Project created by Judith Vincentz Gula

Judy's Way of Design

This exquisite hand-painted batik panel by Jaka creates a wonderful art quilt with doilies, beading, and stitching. For those of you who like to embellish, these batik art panels are terrific and will guide you with the beads, threads, and embellishments.

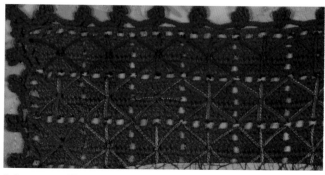
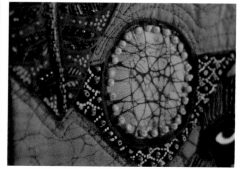

HAND-DYED DOILIES • STITCHING   ECHO QUILTING

CHARMS • BEADING

·+· The Heron ·+·

Project created by Rosalie Lamanna

Judy's Way of Design

The graceful flight of a heron is the work of batik artist Paksi. Beautiful bead work brings the panel to life, adding texture and sparkle. By cutting the panel into squares and adding sashing as you put it back together, it looks as if you're looking through a window.

THE ORIGINAL PANEL

PIECED PANEL

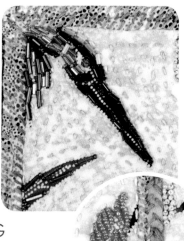

BEADING • STITCHING

·•◆•· Cats in the City ·◆•·

The artist, Mahyar, creates a unique and identifiable pattern and color pallet.
I love his colors, animals, and details. All with wax and dye. Amazing!

Project created by Christine Vinh

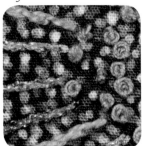

STEM STITCH
FRENCH KNOTS

BEADING

FREE-MOTION QUILTING

⋅⋅✦⋅ Three Sisters ⋅✦⋅⋅

Mayhar's artwork with its bright colors and patterns is hand stitched with WonderFil Eleganza pearl cotton, surrounded with Indian Silks for the borders. There is a little top stitching in the silk borders to hold the three layers together. I wanted the silk to shine.

RICING

Projected created by Judith Vincentz Gula

STEM STITCH

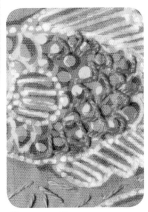

FEATHER STITCH

·•✦•· Dragonfly ·✦·

The dragonfly is a printed panel using wooden printing blocks. The fabric surrounding the dragonfly is hand dyed purple cotton. The center block is bordered by a pop of green and then purple and gold mono printed fabrics with additional wooden printing blocks and gelli plate. The accent hand stitching is done with Tentakulum Threads hand dyed in Germany.

Project created by Liz Kettle

BACK STITCH

RUNNING AND STRAIGHT STITCH

RICING

·•✦• Mermaids ·•✦•

This beautiful mermaid panel by batik artist Suryo is combined with the fish panel by Jaka. Using the motifs of the panels and fabrics, machine stitch to highlight areas but not overwhelm the panels. The blocks are created and assembled in an improvisational, free form style and accented with intuitive quilting.

Project created by Trish Hodge

INTUITIVE QUILTING

INTUITIVE QUILTING

OUTLINE QUILTING

Gallery Tour

Panel by Bambang Dharmo
Project created by Pat Vincentz

Panel by Bambang Dharmo
Project created by Pat Vincentz

Panel by Bambang Dharmo
Project created by Christine Vinh

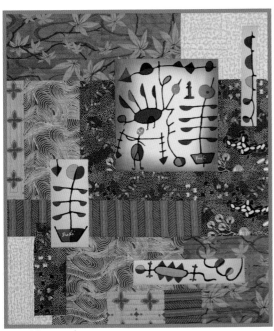

Panel by Rusli
Project created by Christine Vinh
Longarm quilting by Judy Hendrickson

Panel by Rusli
Project created by Christine Vinh
Longarm quilting by Judy Hendrickson

Panel by Rusli
Project created by Liz Kettle

Panel by Ahmed
Project created by Susie Shkolnik

Panel by Ahmed
Project created by Judith Vincentz Gula

Panel by Ahmed
Project created by Marge Holtz

Panel is a vintage handkerchief
Project created by Judith Vincentz Gula

Panel on the back of a quilt
Project created by Trish Hodge

Panel by Bambang Dharmo
Project created by Judith Vincentz Gula

Gallery Tour ·

Panel by Jaka
Project created by Liz Kettle

Panel by Jaka
Project created by Judith Vincentz Gula

Panel by Jaka
Project created by Judith Vincentz Gula

Panel by Mahyar
Project created by Judith Vincentz Gula

Panel by Mahyar
Project created by Judith Vincentz Gula

Panel by Hari Agung
Project created by Cat Mikkleson

About the Author

Judith Vincentz Gula has been a weaver, spinner, fabric dyer, and collector from a very early age. She studied fashion at Radford University, earning degrees in fashion design and business marketing. She has merged all of her many interests and channeled them into making art quilts and samples for her shop, Artistic Artifacts.

Her store was formerly a family business that designed, manufactured, and supplied automotive accessories for European automobiles. Her entrepreneurial spirit allowed her to see the potential in the building when the business closed. The space allowed her to transform her online store into a fiber arts, brick-and-mortar store in Alexandria, Virginia.

*Photo courtesy of
Ann Maas Photography*

Judy travels to shows, conferences, and guilds to share her excitement about what's happening in today's art quilt and fiber world. She is a teacher in her store, offering workshops. Her work has appeared in *A Quilt Block Challenge: Vintage Revisited,* by Mary Kerr; *Creating Celebration Quilts,* by Cyndi Souder; *First-Time Beading on Fabric,* by Liz Kettle; *Modern Handstitching,* by Ruth Chandler; and the Style Section of the *Washington Post.* Her store was featured in *Quilt Sampler Magazine, Spring-Summer 2018* as one of the top ten shops in the United States.

Acknowledgments

Thank you to my family, especially my husband Dave and son Kyle, who have always been with me on my creative journey. To my parents, who continue to be patrons of the arts. The creative artists whose work is included in this book, and the students who infuse me with excitement with their creations. Thanks to Trish and Owen Hodge for introducing Batik Art Panels to us, and the Indonesian Batik Artisans, and Suspriyati Susanto, our partners in creativity.

Ruth Chandler and her wonderful stitches from her book *Modern Hand Stitching*, published by Landauer Publishing, an imprint of Fox Chapel Publishing

Resources

4750 Eisenhower Ave Alexandria, VA 22304
703-823-0202
www.artisticartifacts.com